Victorian Decoupage

SOURCE BOOK

WITH 10 PROJECTS

Projects devised and written by Maggie Philo
Photographed by Debbie Patterson
Original Victorian Scraps from
The Archives of Mamelok Press Ltd
Created by Michelle Lovric

AURUM PRESS

VICTORIAN DECOUPAGE

Text and project design © 1994 Maggie Philo.

Concept and design © 1994 Michelle Lovric,
19 Mercer Street, Covent Garden, London WC2H 9QR.

Victorian Scraps © 1994 Mamelok Press Ltd.

Technical editor: Jean Kievlan.

Book design by Michelle Lovric and Lisa Pentreath.

Printed and bound in Singapore.

First published in Great Britain and the Commonwealth in 1994 by
Aurum Press, 25 Bedford Avenue, London WC1B 3AT.

ISBN No:1-85410-355-5

6 8 10 9 7 5

1997 1998 1996

About the Victorian Scraps....

The Victorian Scraps featured in this book are from the archives of
Mamelok Press Ltd. For further information about the scraps and for
details of all stockists, please write to Mamelok Press Ltd: Northern Way,
Bury St Edmunds, Suffolk IP32 6NJ, England.
Telephone : 01284 762291. Facsimile : 01284 703689.

About the Authors....

Maggie Philo is a highly successful designer, producing a range of beautiful
trays, boxes and furniture. With her extensive knowledge of specialist
paint finishes, she is also in demand as a teacher and interior designer.
She has been profiled in decorating magazines and exhibits regularly at
important interior design shows.This is her second book about decoupage
and she has also made a video about decoupage techniques and ideas.
Maggie is married with five children and lives in Brighton.

Michelle Lovric runs her own company creating specialist books for major
publishers. She has compiled illustrated anthologies, produced kits of
books and cards, written children's stories and designed themed ranges of
cards. Michelle lives and works in Covent Garden, London.

About the Technical Editor...

Jean Kievlan is an accomplished American craft designer and author of over
seventy "how-to" craft instruction booklets and two books about crafts
featuring paper scrap embellishment. Jean is based in Fort Worth, Texas.

ACKNOWLEDGEMENTS:

The editor gratefully acknowledges the assistance of the following companies and
individuals who supplied props for photography in this book:

Glass, china, silverware, wallpapers, fabrics and cushions from Peter Jones, Sloane
Square, London. Peter Jones is part of the John Lewis Partnership.

Decoupaged table on page 6 courtesy of Chelsea Decorative Arts,
3 Biddulph Road, Maida Vale, London W9 1JA.

Christmas wreaths and garlands from The Flowersmith of Covent Garden, London.

Victorian Decoupage

- CONTENTS -

Victorian Decoupage

- A SHORT HISTORY -

The word "scrap" is often used to describe a piece of paper, usually small, printed in colour and often also embossed and diecut. In Victorian times these scraps or "cut-outs" were an integral part of various pastimes for both adults and children, and they remain popular as such in many parts of the world. Meanwhile, the original Victorian scraps have become small vivid emblems of the decorative and sentimental preoccupations of their era, with a romance and appeal all of their own.

Detail from a decoupaged screen in the Mamelok archives

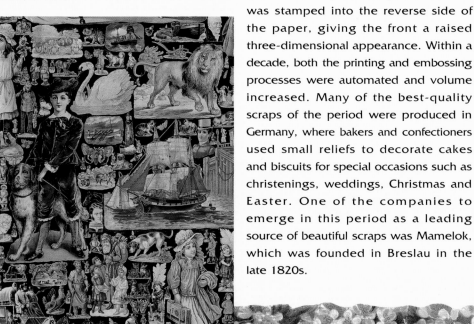

Scraps first appeared at the beginning of the 19th century in the form of simple black-and-white engravings, often later tinted by hand. By the 1820s the scraps had become more elaborate and were sometimes embossed - a process by which a die was stamped into the reverse side of the paper, giving the front a raised three-dimensional appearance. Within a decade, both the printing and embossing processes were automated and volume increased. Many of the best-quality scraps of the period were produced in Germany, where bakers and confectioners used small reliefs to decorate cakes and biscuits for special occasions such as christenings, weddings, Christmas and Easter. One of the companies to emerge in this period as a leading source of beautiful scraps was Mamelok, which was founded in Breslau in the late 1820s.

In 1837, the first year of Queen Victoria's reign, came the invention of the colour-printing process known as chromolithography and scrap manufacturers were quick to apply the new technology to their products. Now brightly coloured and embossed scraps were sold in sheets with the relief stamped out to the approximate shape of the image. These pre-cut scraps were connected by small strips of paper to keep them in place.

Pages from a scrapbook in the Mamelok archives

The laborious task of cutting out small pictures was thus removed, and sales of scraps began to increase significantly. Collections of scraps were pasted into specially-produced albums, together with other decorated paper items such as calling cards, food wrappers and pictures from magazines and catalogues. Scrap collectors would fill the pages of their albums with pictures grouped in themes. Often the pictures would be supplemented by personal notes, lines of poetry or dedications from friends and relatives.

The Victorians delighted in romanticism and sentimentality. Sought-after subjects for scraps included angelic-looking children, fashionably-dressed ladies, birds, butterflies, pets, angels and fans. Also popular were military and naval themes and scraps depicting Victorian pastimes such as the circus and outings to the seaside.

Before long, scraps were being pasted into autograph books and diaries, on calling cards, friendship cards and, not surprisingly, they were also used to create the most unashamedly romantic Valentines. These cards were often composed from an extravagant array of diverse materials such as paper lace, embossed gold foil, ribbons, lace, fresh flowers and feathers, with the scraps as the main focal point.

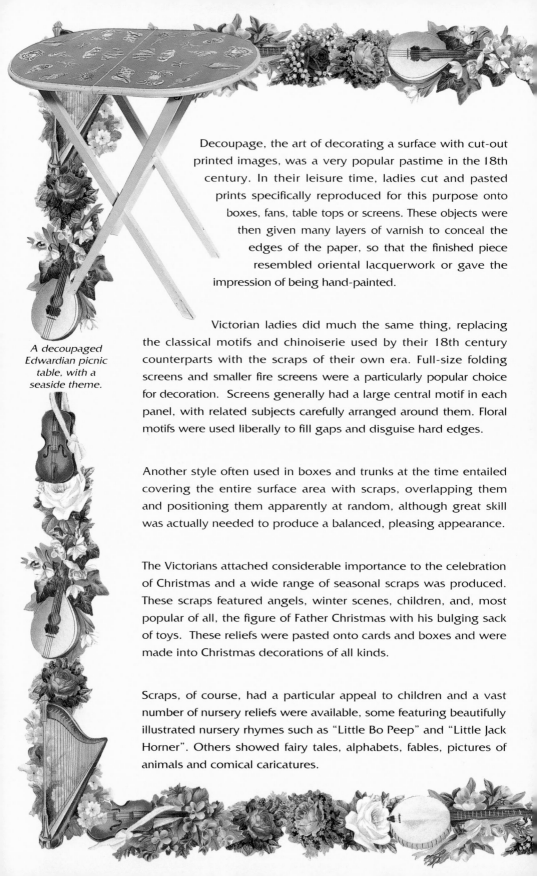

Decoupage, the art of decorating a surface with cut-out printed images, was a very popular pastime in the 18th century. In their leisure time, ladies cut and pasted prints specifically reproduced for this purpose onto boxes, fans, table tops or screens. These objects were then given many layers of varnish to conceal the edges of the paper, so that the finished piece resembled oriental lacquerwork or gave the impression of being hand-painted.

A decoupaged Edwardian picnic table, with a seaside theme.

Victorian ladies did much the same thing, replacing the classical motifs and chinoiserie used by their 18th century counterparts with the scraps of their own era. Full-size folding screens and smaller fire screens were a particularly popular choice for decoration. Screens generally had a large central motif in each panel, with related subjects carefully arranged around them. Floral motifs were used liberally to fill gaps and disguise hard edges.

Another style often used in boxes and trunks at the time entailed covering the entire surface area with scraps, overlapping them and positioning them apparently at random, although great skill was actually needed to produce a balanced, pleasing appearance.

The Victorians attached considerable importance to the celebration of Christmas and a wide range of seasonal scraps was produced. These scraps featured angels, winter scenes, children, and, most popular of all, the figure of Father Christmas with his bulging sack of toys. These reliefs were pasted onto cards and boxes and were made into Christmas decorations of all kinds.

Scraps, of course, had a particular appeal to children and a vast number of nursery reliefs were available, some featuring beautifully illustrated nursery rhymes such as "Little Bo Peep" and "Little Jack Horner". Others showed fairy tales, alphabets, fables, pictures of animals and comical caricatures.

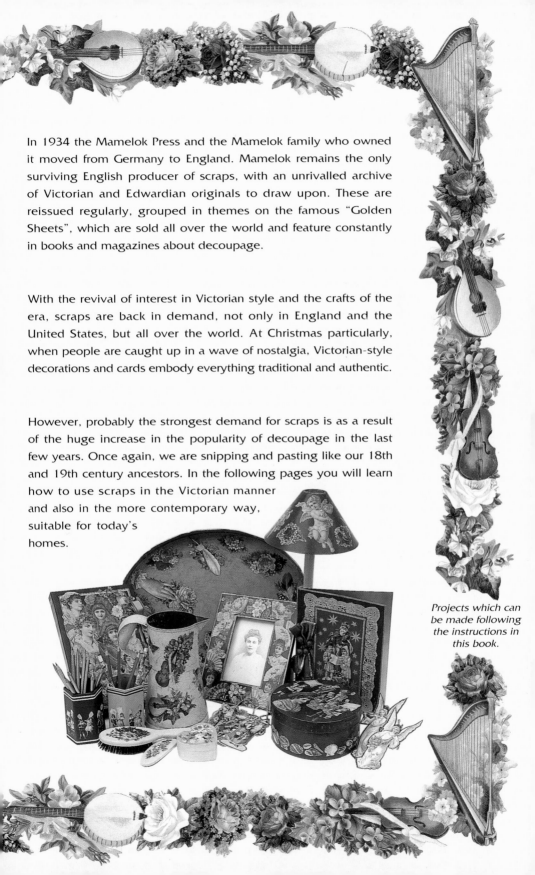

In 1934 the Mamelok Press and the Mamelok family who owned it moved from Germany to England. Mamelok remains the only surviving English producer of scraps, with an unrivalled archive of Victorian and Edwardian originals to draw upon. These are reissued regularly, grouped in themes on the famous "Golden Sheets", which are sold all over the world and feature constantly in books and magazines about decoupage.

With the revival of interest in Victorian style and the crafts of the era, scraps are back in demand, not only in England and the United States, but all over the world. At Christmas particularly, when people are caught up in a wave of nostalgia, Victorian-style decorations and cards embody everything traditional and authentic.

However, probably the strongest demand for scraps is as a result of the huge increase in the popularity of decoupage in the last few years. Once again, we are snipping and pasting like our 18th and 19th century ancestors. In the following pages you will learn how to use scraps in the Victorian manner and also in the more contemporary way, suitable for today's homes.

Projects which can be made following the instructions in this book.

- MATERIALS -

The following materials are used for most of the projects in this book. Additional materials specific to a particular project are listed in the relevant sections.

MANICURE SCISSORS

SMALL CRAFT KNIFE OR SCALPEL

CUTTING MAT OR THICK CARD

PASTE OR P.V.A. GLUE

HOUSEHOLD SPONGE

WATER-BASED SATIN ACRYLIC VARNISH

BRUSHES FOR GLUING, PAINTING AND VARNISHING

FINE GRADE SANDPAPER

ACRYLIC VARNISH

CRAQUELEUR KIT

GILT CREAM

BROWN WAX

RUBBER ROLLER

RAW UMBER PAINTS

GLUES

PAINTS

CLEAR
SHELLAC

SCISSORS AND SMALL
CRAFT KNIFE OR SCALPEL

PRIMERS

- TECHNIQUES -

You can stick your Victorian scraps onto almost any surface, but if you are going to apply several layers of varnish you will need to choose an item that is rigid. Junk shops can be a wonderful source for suitable pieces and hardware and craft stores are good, too. Items similar to those in this book can be found easily and indeed you may already have some that are just waiting to be given this very special treatment and a new lease of life.

- PREPARATION OF SURFACES -

Some surfaces need no special preparation but others will need to be prepared carefully to produce a professional-looking piece of work.

WOOD. Old wood that has been painted or varnished must be cleaned and sanded well with a medium grade sand paper and any holes and cracks should be filled. Before painting new wood, seal the surface with a wood primer, shellac sanding sealer or water-based acrylic sealer.

ENAMEL AND TIN. It is very important to treat the rust you are likely to find on old enamel. If you don't, it will eventually eat its way through the paint and spoil all your hard work. First of all, remove any loose or flaking pieces with coarse grade sandpaper then treat the area with a proprietary rust-proofing agent and paint the item with an oil-based primer. Alternatively, use an all-in-one rust-proofer and primer according to the manufacturers' instructions. Paint tin and new enamel with an oil-based metal primer.

GALVANIZED METAL. Weathered galvanized metal that is free of rust needs only to be cleaned thoroughly with detergent and water before it is ready to paint. Alternatively, you may wash the items with a mixture of vinegar and water (half vinegar, half water). If there are signs of rust, treat as for rusting enamel. New galvanized metal should be painted with a primer for galvanized metal surfaces according to the manufacturers' instructions, to provide a surface to which paint can adhere.

PAPER AND CARD. Paper and card that are going to be painted should first be sealed with clear shellac applied with either a brush or a cloth.

- PAINTING THE BACKGROUND -

Water-based emulsion or latex/acrylic paints have been used for all the painted projects in this book. Tints of dark green, burgundy and brown, shades associated with Victorian decorative schemes, make particularly good backgrounds for the scraps. Muted pastels also look good, but very bright primary shades would probably not be an appropriate choice. You will always need to apply at least two coats of paint, letting the first one dry before applying the second.

- CUTTING OUT THE SCRAPS -

As the scraps have been partially cut out, most of the hard work has been done, but you will need to cut away the connecting strips. A sharp pair of manicure scissors is essential for this, either with a straight or curved edge, depending which you find the most comfortable. To give your work an extra quality you will also need to cut out some internal areas of background paper that do not form part of the design: for example, the areas underneath the arms of the children on the seaside scraps. This is best done with a sharp craft or scalpel knife using a cutting mat or a piece of stiff card to cut on. Some people find small scissors easier to handle than a knife.

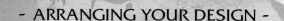

- ARRANGING YOUR DESIGN -

Arranging the scraps on a flat surface, such as a hairbrush or tray, is fairly straightforward, but designs on vertical surfaces and those that overlap are slightly more tricky. In both cases you will need to spray the back of your scraps with a repositionable glue or attach a re-usable adhesive before arranging them in a balanced design. When you have an overlapping arrangement of cut-outs, like those on the picture frame and photo album in this book, start by placing your scraps at the top of the item and gradually work down the surface. Unfortunately, you will need to remove these before permanently gluing them into place, but before you do so, mark their position lightly with chalk or pencil on the surface so that you can reposition them accurately.

You may want to vary the scrap arrangements used in this book so that they fit a particular background or reflect your own sense of style. If this is the case, it is a good idea to cut out more motifs than you need, so that you can experiment with different designs.

- GLUING -

You can use either a simple paste glue or a P.V.A. adhesive for gluing the scraps in place. Paste glue was used for all the projects in this book, apart from the Christmas ones, and because it is slower drying than P.V.A., you have a minute or two to change your mind about the position of a scrap if you are not quite happy with the placement. You will find it much easier and cleaner if you apply the glue to the surface you are decorating rather than to the back of the scrap. Stick each motif down separately by brushing the glue onto the appropriate area, placing the scrap over it and pressing down firmly with your fingertips, working any bubbles of air out from the middle of the paper towards the edge. You may find a lino-printing roller a useful tool for eliminating air bubbles when you are working on a flat surface, but it is by no means essential. If you have used a paste glue, leave your work to dry for about half an hour before cleaning off the excess glue with a damp sponge. However, P.V.A. glue should be wiped from the surface right away. Let your project dry thoroughly for a further two hours.

- VARNISHING -

Before varnishing, check that all your edges are firmly stuck down and re-glue any that are not. Also make sure that you are working in a dust-free area and that you are wearing clothing that will not shed hairs or fibres. The next stage is to apply between three and twelve coats of varnish, depending on the project and the quality of finish you require. A water-based acrylic varnish is best used for this and under normal conditions you should be able to apply four or five coats in a day. Do make sure you use a varnish with a satin finish rather than a matte one as the latter contains a matting agent that will make the varnish appear cloudy after you have put on several coats. Start by applying a thin even layer using a flat varnish brush for preference, or, if you do not have one, you can use an ordinary household paint brush. Let it dry for at least two hours before brushing on the next coat. To achieve a really smooth finish on your work, you will need to sand back the second-to-last layer of varnish with a fine grade sandpaper before applying the final coat. However, you should never do this unless you have used at least six coats of varnish or you will damage the scraps and reveal the white edges of the paper.

- WAXING AND FINISHING -

A final coat of satin varnish is a perfectly satisfactory finish but if it is a little too shiny for your taste, you can rub it down with fine steel wool. You may like to finish your work with the crackle varnish technique that was used for the musical jug in this book and this is described on page 33. Several other projects have been finished with an antique or brown staining wax. This is a very simple but effective way of giving a piece the mellow look and feel of an antique. If you decide on this, the final coat of varnish you apply should be rubbed down with fine steel wool to prepare the best surface for the wax. Simply apply the wax evenly with a soft cloth and let it dry for about half an hour before buffing to a shine with a clean cloth.

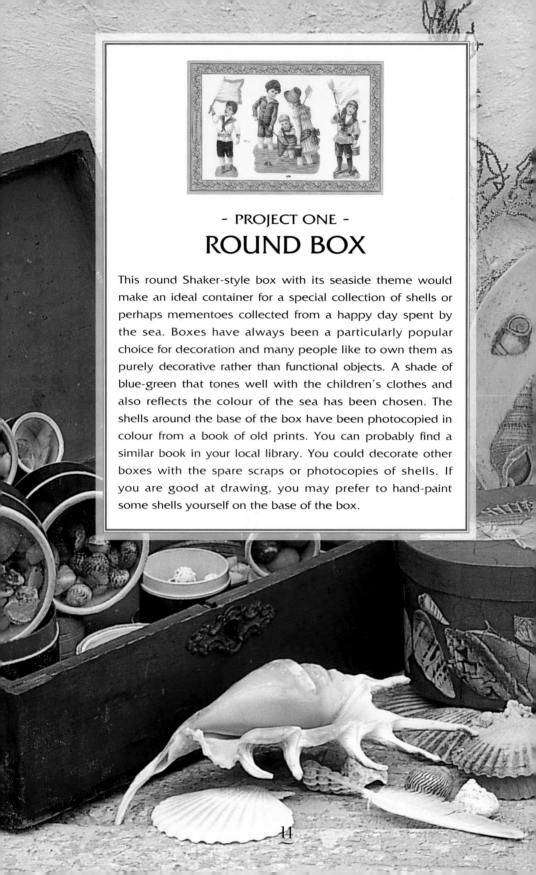

- PROJECT ONE -
ROUND BOX

This round Shaker-style box with its seaside theme would make an ideal container for a special collection of shells or perhaps mementoes collected from a happy day spent by the sea. Boxes have always been a particularly popular choice for decoration and many people like to own them as purely decorative rather than functional objects. A shade of blue-green that tones well with the children's clothes and also reflects the colour of the sea has been chosen. The shells around the base of the box have been photocopied in colour from a book of old prints. You can probably find a similar book in your local library. You could decorate other boxes with the spare scraps or photocopies of shells. If you are good at drawing, you may prefer to hand-paint some shells yourself on the base of the box.

YOU WILL NEED

Items from the basic materials kit on page 8 plus

Round wooden box
Scraps from Sheets 2, 38
Colour photocopy of shells (OPTIONAL)
Brown shellac
Methylated spirits for cleaning shellac brush
Blue-green paint - emulsion, latex or acrylic
Repositionable glue
Medium brown wax
Very fine steel wool
Soft cloth

ROUND BOX
STEP-BY-STEP

STEP 1

Seal the inside of the box by brushing with a brown shellac and paint the outside of the base and lid with two coats of a blue-green paint. You may find this easier if you apply the paint in two stages starting with the sides, and then, when these are dry, painting the top and bottom surfaces.

STEP 2

Carefully cut out the scraps and arrange them on the surface of the lid. When you have an arrangement you like, glue the scraps firmly in place, smoothing any bubbles of air out from the middle of the paper towards the edges.

STEP 3 (OPTIONAL)

Cut out the photocopies of shells, cutting more than you think you will need, so that you can experiment with different designs. Spray the back of each with repositionable glue. To ensure a balanced arrangement, take a few similarly-shaped shells, and place them around the base of the box, leaving an equal space between each one. Then arrange more shells between each section. Six scallop shells were used on this box with four other shells placed in the space between each one. Finally, glue the shells firmly in place.

STEP 4

Brush the whole of the exterior of the box with two coats of satin acrylic varnish. Then continue to varnish over the scraps on the top of the lid and the sides of the base only. After about ten layers, smooth back the second-to-last layer with sandpaper. Apply a final coat of varnish and when this is thoroughly dry, take the gloss off the surface with very fine steel wool. Then give the box a coat of medium brown wax, rubbed on with a soft cloth.

- PROJECT TWO -
PICTURE FRAME

You will need to choose a frame with a flat surface that is wide enough to take the fans, ladies and flowers which have been used here. Although we started with a new and very modern looking frame, the decorative treatment has resulted in a finished item that certainly would not have looked out of place in a Victorian household. A gilt cream has been rubbed over the green paint on the edges of the frame and this simple technique is particularly effective when it is used over a dark shade of paint. As an alternative to the dark green and gold frame, you could use a dark cream coloured paint and antique it, following the instructions for the tray (page 25): this is the technique used to finish the frame in the background of the picture opposite. Although a picture frame has been used here, a mirror frame would be equally successful and look very pretty hung on a sitting room or bedroom wall.

YOU WILL NEED

Items from the basic materials kit on page 8 plus

Scraps from Sheets 13, 14, 70, 71, 89
Wooden picture frame
Medium grade sandpaper
Dark green paint - emulsion, latex or acrylic
Masking tape
Gilt cream or Antique Gold Rub 'n' Buff ™
(American Art Clay Co.)
Repositionable glue
Antique wax
Very fine steel wool
Cotton buds or swabs
Soft cloth
Chalk

PICTURE FRAME
STEP-BY-STEP

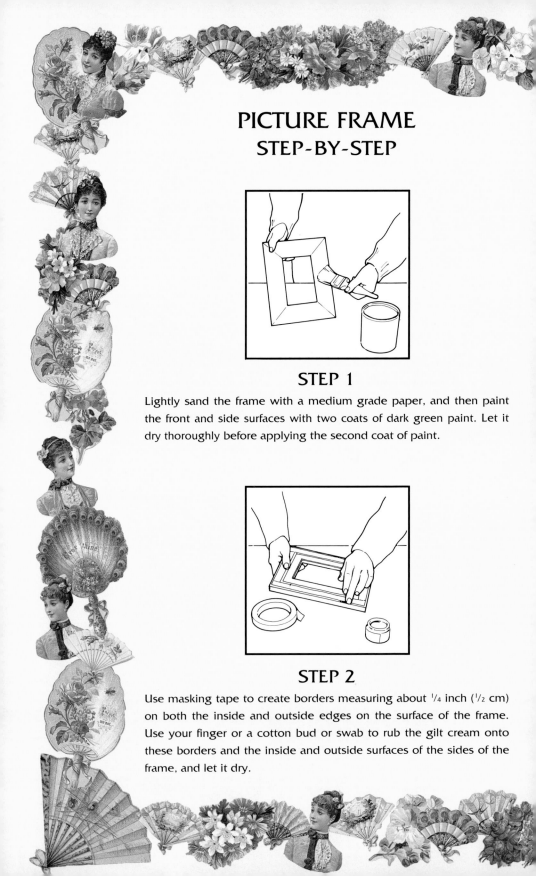

STEP 1

Lightly sand the frame with a medium grade paper, and then paint the front and side surfaces with two coats of dark green paint. Let it dry thoroughly before applying the second coat of paint.

STEP 2

Use masking tape to create borders measuring about ¼ inch (½ cm) on both the inside and outside edges on the surface of the frame. Use your finger or a cotton bud or swab to rub the gilt cream onto these borders and the inside and outside surfaces of the sides of the frame, and let it dry.

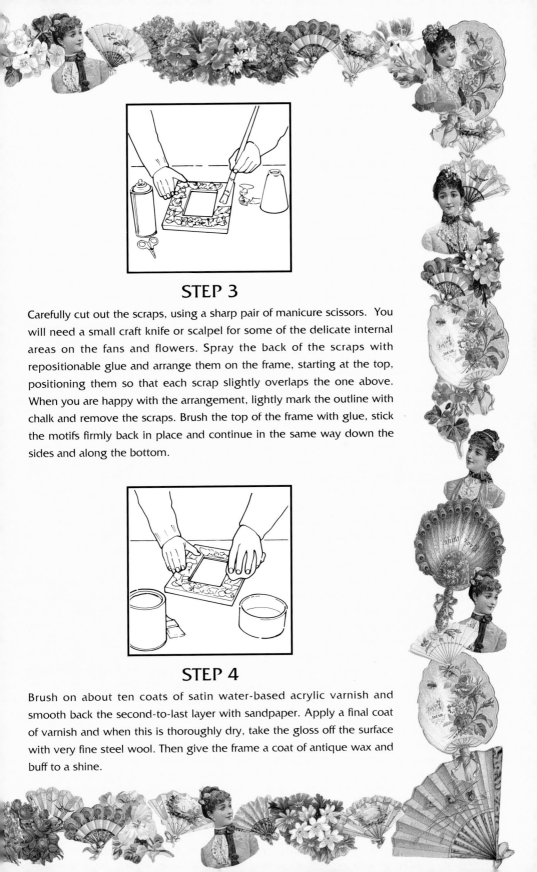

STEP 3

Carefully cut out the scraps, using a sharp pair of manicure scissors. You will need a small craft knife or scalpel for some of the delicate internal areas on the fans and flowers. Spray the back of the scraps with repositionable glue and arrange them on the frame, starting at the top, positioning them so that each scrap slightly overlaps the one above. When you are happy with the arrangement, lightly mark the outline with chalk and remove the scraps. Brush the top of the frame with glue, stick the motifs firmly back in place and continue in the same way down the sides and along the bottom.

STEP 4

Brush on about ten coats of satin water-based acrylic varnish and smooth back the second-to-last layer with sandpaper. Apply a final coat of varnish and when this is thoroughly dry, take the gloss off the surface with very fine steel wool. Then give the frame a coat of antique wax and buff to a shine.

- PROJECT THREE -
TRAY

This tray, with its design of graceful hands reaching out with their offerings of posies, would make a wonderful gift for a very good friend. Set it with fine china and you have the perfect choice for afternoon tea or a romantic breakfast in bed. The tray has been given an antique look with a brown paint brushed over the surface, and the pretty scalloped edge has been highlighted with gold. A cream paint would make a very good alternative choice and would match most kitchen or dining room decor schemes, so don't hide your tray away in a cupboard when it's not in use, but display it on a table or sideboard instead.

YOU WILL NEED

Items from the basic materials kit on page 8 plus

M.D.F. (medium density fibreboard) or wood tray
(prepared according to the instructions on page 10)

Scraps from Sheets 20, 79, 89, 90

Light green paint - emulsion, latex or acrylic

Raw umber powder pigment and white emulsion (latex)
paint or raw umber artists' acrylic paint

Paper towel

Medium brown wax

Very fine steel wool

Soft cloth

Gilt cream or Rub 'n' Buff ™ (American Art Clay Co.)

Oil-based varnish (matte) (OPTIONAL)

Cotton buds or swabs

TRAY
STEP-BY-STEP

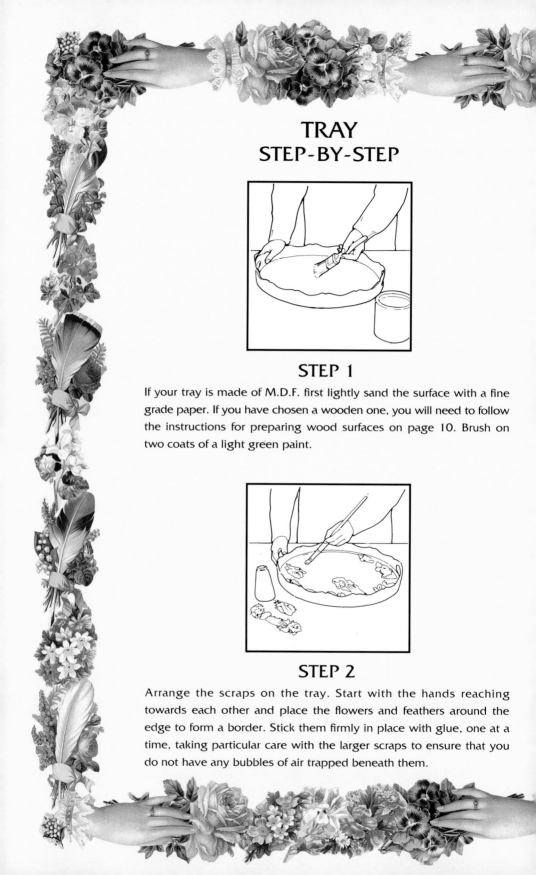

STEP 1

If your tray is made of M.D.F. first lightly sand the surface with a fine grade paper. If you have chosen a wooden one, you will need to follow the instructions for preparing wood surfaces on page 10. Brush on two coats of a light green paint.

STEP 2

Arrange the scraps on the tray. Start with the hands reaching towards each other and place the flowers and feathers around the edge to form a border. Stick them firmly in place with glue, one at a time, taking particular care with the larger scraps to ensure that you do not have any bubbles of air trapped beneath them.

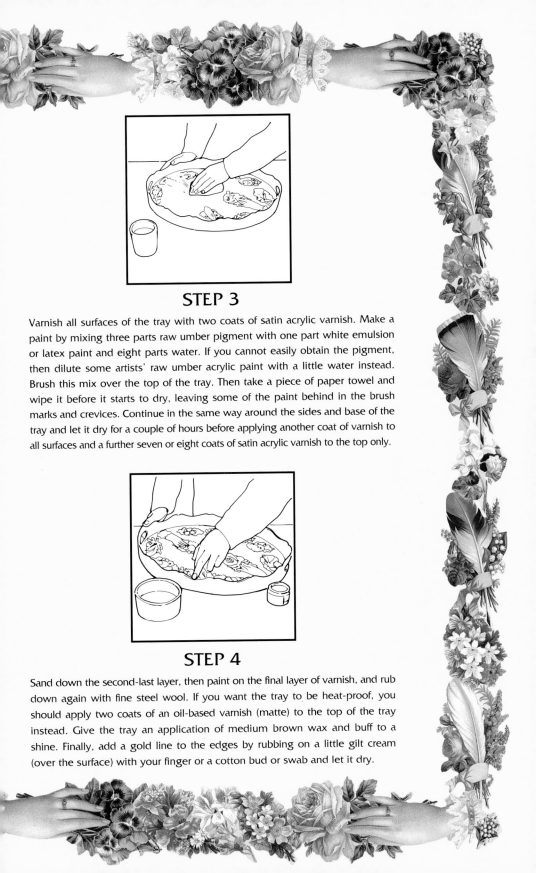

STEP 3

Varnish all surfaces of the tray with two coats of satin acrylic varnish. Make a paint by mixing three parts raw umber pigment with one part white emulsion or latex paint and eight parts water. If you cannot easily obtain the pigment, then dilute some artists' raw umber acrylic paint with a little water instead. Brush this mix over the top of the tray. Then take a piece of paper towel and wipe it before it starts to dry, leaving some of the paint behind in the brush marks and crevices. Continue in the same way around the sides and base of the tray and let it dry for a couple of hours before applying another coat of varnish to all surfaces and a further seven or eight coats of satin acrylic varnish to the top only.

STEP 4

Sand down the second-last layer, then paint on the final layer of varnish, and rub down again with fine steel wool. If you want the tray to be heat-proof, you should apply two coats of an oil-based varnish (matte) to the top of the tray instead. Give the tray an application of medium brown wax and buff to a shine. Finally, add a gold line to the edges by rubbing on a little gilt cream (over the surface) with your finger or a cotton bud or swab and let it dry.

- PROJECT FOUR -
CANDLE-SHADE

This combination of delicate cherubs and red roses set against a deep red background makes a wonderfully romantic shade. Place it over a crystal candlestick and you have the perfect illumination for a Saint Valentine's Day dinner for two. If you cannot find a metal shade, you could use a flame-proof paper one and seal it with shellac before painting it. As an alternative to the red used here, a shade of dusty pink would be a very pretty and an equally appropriate choice for the background. The inside of the candle-shade should be painted a paler tint so that it reflects the light from the flame. A coat of wax has been applied over the layers of varnish to give the finished shade extra depth and a subtle sheen.

YOU WILL NEED

Items from the basic materials kit on page 8 plus

Metal candle-shade
Scraps from Sheets 60, 76
Oil-based metal primer
Deep red and cream paint
- emulsion, latex or acrylic
Repositionable glue
Medium brown wax
Soft cloth
Very fine steel wool
Detergent or vinegar and water wash

Page from a Victorian Scrapbook in Mamelok arch

CANDLE-SHADE
STEP-BY-STEP

STEP 1

First wash the shade either with detergent or a vinegar and water wash (half vinegar, half water) and dry thoroughly. Prime the shade by painting it with one or two coats of an oil-based metal primer before applying the deep red paint to the outside. You will probably find you need three coats to give a good cover when you are using shades of red. Brush two coats of a cream paint onto the inside of the shade.

STEP 2

Carefully cut out the scraps, using a sharp pair of manicure scissors and a small craft knife or scalpel for the internal areas of the cherub motifs. Next spray the backs of the scraps with repositionable glue. Arrange them around the shade, making sure that you have a balanced design by looking carefully at the spaces you leave between the scraps. Remove one scrap at a time, brush the shade with glue, and then stick the scrap back in place, smoothing out from the middle of the paper towards the edges.

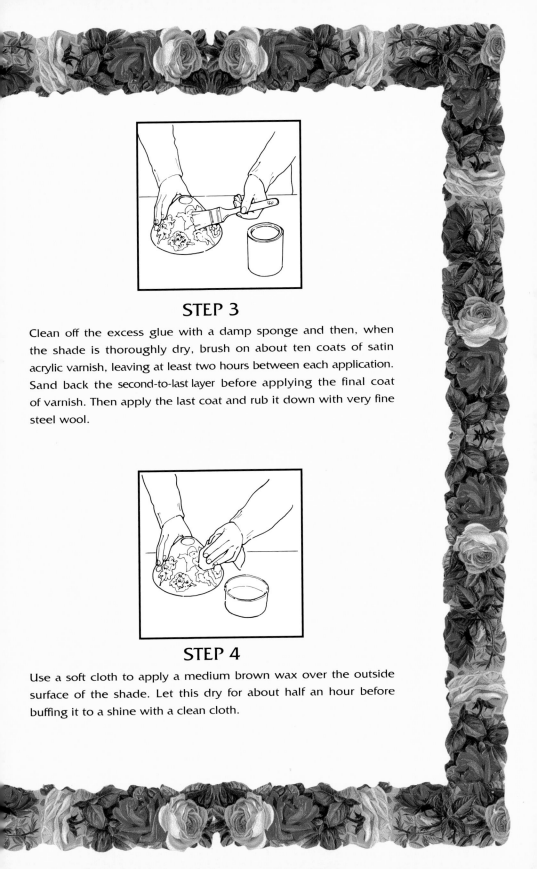

STEP 3

Clean off the excess glue with a damp sponge and then, when the shade is thoroughly dry, brush on about ten coats of satin acrylic varnish, leaving at least two hours between each application. Sand back the second-to-last layer before applying the final coat of varnish. Then apply the last coat and rub it down with very fine steel wool.

STEP 4

Use a soft cloth to apply a medium brown wax over the outside surface of the shade. Let this dry for about half an hour before buffing it to a shine with a clean cloth.

- PROJECT FIVE -

CRAQUELEUR MUSICAL JUG

The term 'craqueleur' is used to describe a finished appearance that resembles cracked and aged porcelain. This technique can be applied to any object, but seems particularly appropriate for the rustic-style jug illustrated here. You can find other galvanized steel objects - hip baths, buckets and watering cans, for example - in junk shops or you can buy them new from hardware stores. Jugs like this one were originally used on farms and look wonderful filled with a bunch of fresh flowers. If you want to put yours to a similar use, leave the inside unpainted, or, if you do paint it, protect the inside by placing the flowers in a jam jar inside the jug.

YOU WILL NEED

*Items from the basic materials kit
on page 8 plus*

Galvanized jug
Scraps from Sheets 76, 77
Primer for galvanized metal
Cream paint - emulsion, latex or acrylic
Repositionable glue
Two-part crackle varnish kit
$\frac{1}{2}$ - 1 inch (1 - 2$\frac{1}{2}$ cm) soft-haired brush
Raw umber artists' oil paint
Paper towel and soft cloth
White spirit (mineral spirits)
Oil-based varnish (matte)
Antique wax
Detergent or vinegar and water wash

CRAQUELEUR MUSICAL JUG
STEP-BY-STEP

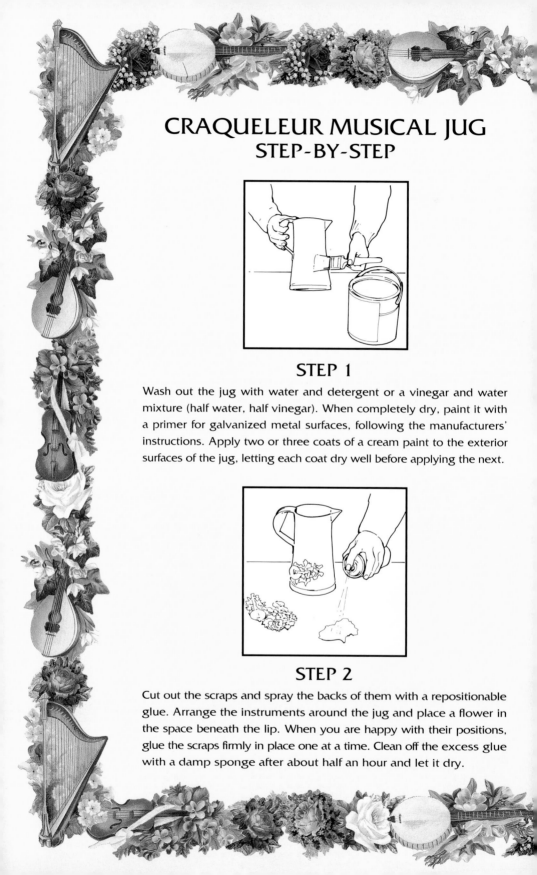

STEP 1

Wash out the jug with water and detergent or a vinegar and water mixture (half water, half vinegar). When completely dry, paint it with a primer for galvanized metal surfaces, following the manufacturers' instructions. Apply two or three coats of a cream paint to the exterior surfaces of the jug, letting each coat dry well before applying the next.

STEP 2

Cut out the scraps and spray the backs of them with a repositionable glue. Arrange the instruments around the jug and place a flower in the space beneath the lip. When you are happy with their positions, glue the scraps firmly in place one at a time. Clean off the excess glue with a damp sponge after about half an hour and let it dry.

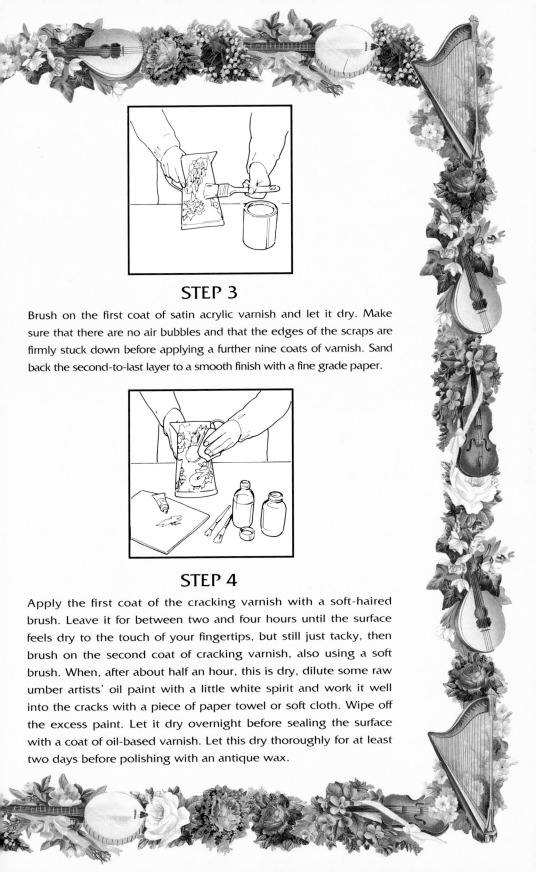

STEP 3

Brush on the first coat of satin acrylic varnish and let it dry. Make sure that there are no air bubbles and that the edges of the scraps are firmly stuck down before applying a further nine coats of varnish. Sand back the second-to-last layer to a smooth finish with a fine grade paper.

STEP 4

Apply the first coat of the cracking varnish with a soft-haired brush. Leave it for between two and four hours until the surface feels dry to the touch of your fingertips, but still just tacky, then brush on the second coat of cracking varnish, also using a soft brush. When, after about half an hour, this is dry, dilute some raw umber artists' oil paint with a little white spirit and work it well into the cracks with a piece of paper towel or soft cloth. Wipe off the excess paint. Let it dry overnight before sealing the surface with a coat of oil-based varnish. Let this dry thoroughly for at least two days before polishing with an antique wax.

- PROJECT SIX -
PENCIL HOLDER

This pencil holder would make a lovely gift for a child and is sure to be much appreciated, especially if it is filled with pretty pens and pencils. This is not a very difficult project and you might like to provide all the pieces in a kit so that the child could make it for him or herself. The little sailor suits these Victorian children are wearing are reflected in the paper stripes which have been added to the top and bottom of the holder. Shades of blue have been chosen to further highlight the naval theme, but you could use white stripes on a dark blue background as a striking alternative.

YOU WILL NEED

Items from the basic materials kit on page 8 plus

Cardboard pencil holder

Scraps from Sheet 7

Clear shellac

Methylated spirits or denatured alcohol for cleaning shellac brush

Steel ruler

Sheet of dark blue paper

Light blue paint - emulsion, latex or acrylic

Repositionable glue

STEP 1

Brush a clear shellac onto both the inside and outside surfaces of the holder to seal it, and when it is dry apply two coats of a light blue paint.

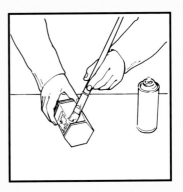

STEP 3

Cut out the figures of the children and spray the back of each scrap with repositionable glue. Arrange them around the surface of the holder, a little way above the blue stripe, then remove one or two scraps at a time, brush the glue on in their place and stick them firmly back into position, making sure you do not have any bubbles of trapped air. Clean off the excess glue with a damp sponge after about half an hour, then let it dry thoroughly for two more hours.

STEP 2

Using a steel ruler and a small craft knife or scalpel, cut three dark blue paper borders, each about 1/8 inch (3 mm) wide and glue these in position, placing two at the top and one around the base of the holder.

STEP 4

Apply between ten and twelve coats of satin acrylic varnish, leaving at least two hours between each coat before applying the next. Sand back the second-to-last layer with a fine grade paper for a nice smooth finish.

- PROJECT SEVEN -
PHOTO ALBUM

The photo album in this project is a good example of how a very ordinary and inexpensive item can be transformed into something that is unique and special, with the addition of a few scraps, a gold border and some pretty ribbon. Because the image area is made from layers of overlapping paper, you will need to take particular care at the gluing stage, making sure that all the edges of the scraps are firmly stuck down. You can stick the scraps down in fairly quick succession as you don't need to wait for one to dry before gluing the next over it. The album has been given an authentic Victorian look with three layers of brown shellac rubbed over the surface to yellow and age it..

YOU WILL NEED

*Items from the basic
materials kit on page 8 plus*

Photo album
Scraps from Sheets 2, 19, 25, 26, 37
Gold fine-tip marking pen
Ruler
Repositionable glue
White chalk
Brown shellac
³/₄ yard (70 cm) gold ribbon
Soft cotton cloth
Sheet of white paper (OPTIONAL)

PHOTO ALBUM
STEP-BY-STEP

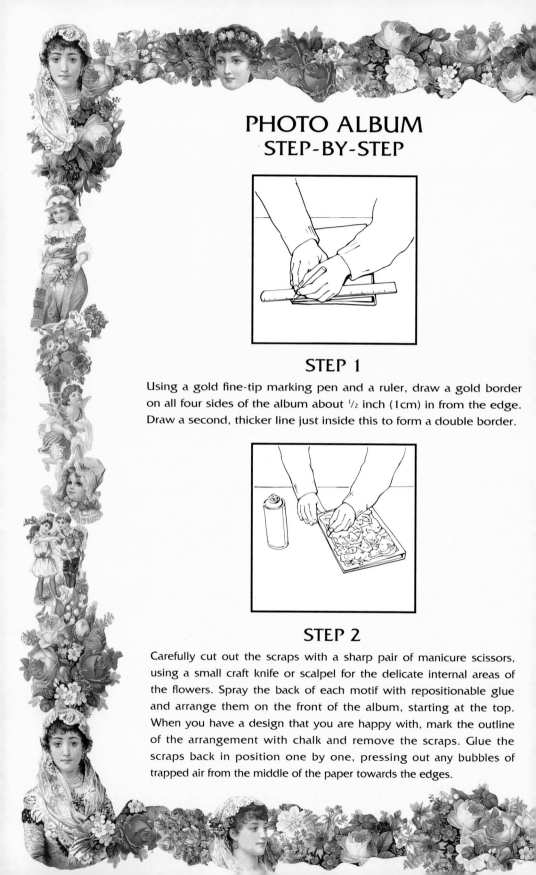

STEP 1

Using a gold fine-tip marking pen and a ruler, draw a gold border on all four sides of the album about $1/2$ inch (1cm) in from the edge. Draw a second, thicker line just inside this to form a double border.

STEP 2

Carefully cut out the scraps with a sharp pair of manicure scissors, using a small craft knife or scalpel for the delicate internal areas of the flowers. Spray the back of each motif with repositionable glue and arrange them on the front of the album, starting at the top. When you have a design that you are happy with, mark the outline of the arrangement with chalk and remove the scraps. Glue the scraps back in position one by one, pressing out any bubbles of trapped air from the middle of the paper towards the edges.

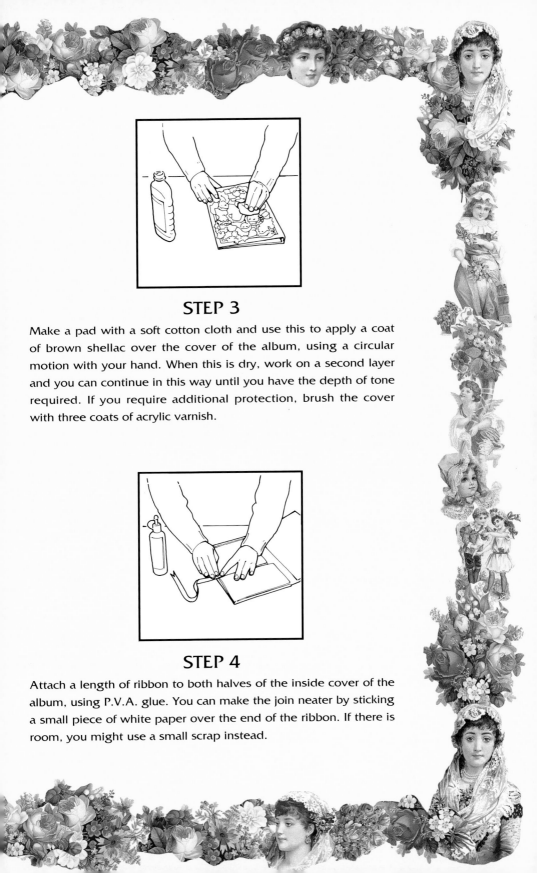

STEP 3

Make a pad with a soft cotton cloth and use this to apply a coat of brown shellac over the cover of the album, using a circular motion with your hand. When this is dry, work on a second layer and you can continue in this way until you have the depth of tone required. If you require additional protection, brush the cover with three coats of acrylic varnish.

STEP 4

Attach a length of ribbon to both halves of the inside cover of the album, using P.V.A. glue. You can make the join neater by sticking a small piece of white paper over the end of the ribbon. If there is room, you might use a small scrap instead.

- PROJECT EIGHT -
HAIRBRUSH

This is by far the most simple project in this book but none-the-less desirable for it. If you want an extra personal touch, you could add a name or initials on the handle either by hand or perhaps with transfer lettering using an appropriate type face such as Old English. The brush has been left unpainted, not only because the natural texture of the wood is very attractive but also because the bristles come directly out from the wood, making it difficult to do otherwise! However, if your brush has a separate rubber or plastic base, you could paint it, if you wish. You might like to use some of the extra scraps from the same sheet to decorate other small items for your dressing table, like the hairclip and little heart-shaped box shown in the picture. A mirror would also be a very good choice and add a lovely touch.

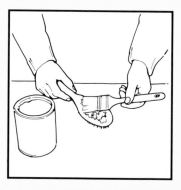

STEP 1

Carefully cut away the excess paper around the scrap using a sharp pair of manicure scissors. Apply glue to the surface of the brush and stick the pansy motif firmly into position, making sure all the edges are well stuck down and that there is no air trapped beneath. After about half an hour, clean off the excess glue with a damp sponge and leave the brush to dry thoroughly for a further two hours.

STEP 2

If you wish to add a name or initials to the handle, do this now, then apply between three and ten coats of satin acrylic varnish to the top of the brush, depending on the quality of finish that you are happy with. If you apply more than six coats, smooth back the second-to-last layer with a fine grade sandpaper. Your final coat of varnish can be whatever finish you prefer.

YOU WILL NEED

*Items from the basic materials kit
on page 8 plus*

Wooden hair brush

Scrap from Sheet 90

Water-based acrylic varnish (matte)
- OPTIONAL

- PROJECT NINE -

VERY SPECIAL
CHRISTMAS CARD

This is a card to make for someone very special, like your mother or your best friend. You can be sure it will stand out among the other cards on a mantlepiece and, when Christmas is over, it will be saved and cherished. If you cannot find a gold doily, spray a white one with gold paint instead. A tartan ribbon would look just as nice as the green and gold one used here and you could make the card even more special by decorating the back or the inside of the card with the other Christmas scene from the same sheet of scraps. If you cannot bear to give this card away, use it instead to contain your Christmas Day menu. If you write the menu on a separate piece of paper, you can attach it temporarily to the inside of the card, and use it again year after year.

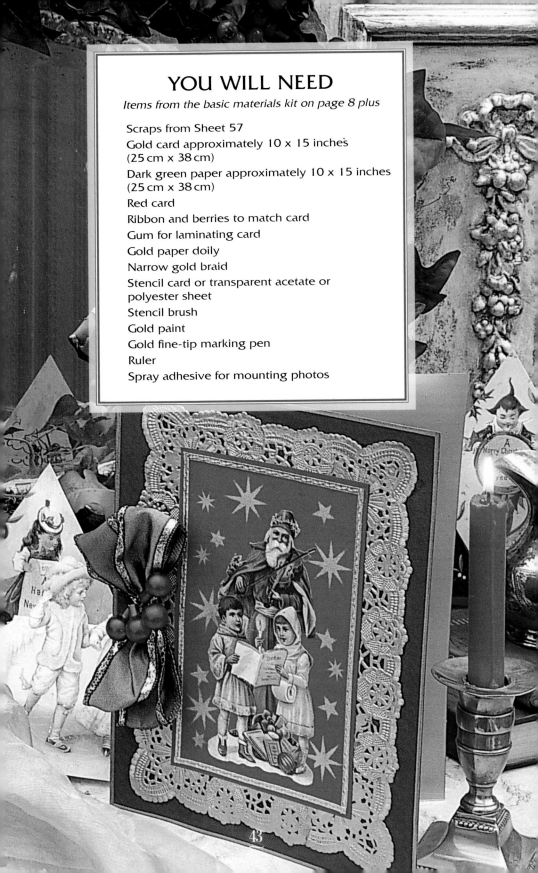

YOU WILL NEED

Items from the basic materials kit on page 8 plus

Scraps from Sheet 57

Gold card approximately 10 x 15 inches
(25 cm x 38 cm)

Dark green paper approximately 10 x 15 inches
(25 cm x 38 cm)

Red card

Ribbon and berries to match card

Gum for laminating card

Gold paper doily

Narrow gold braid

Stencil card or transparent acetate or
polyester sheet

Stencil brush

Gold paint

Gold fine-tip marking pen

Ruler

Spray adhesive for mounting photos

CHRISTMAS CARD
STEP-BY-STEP

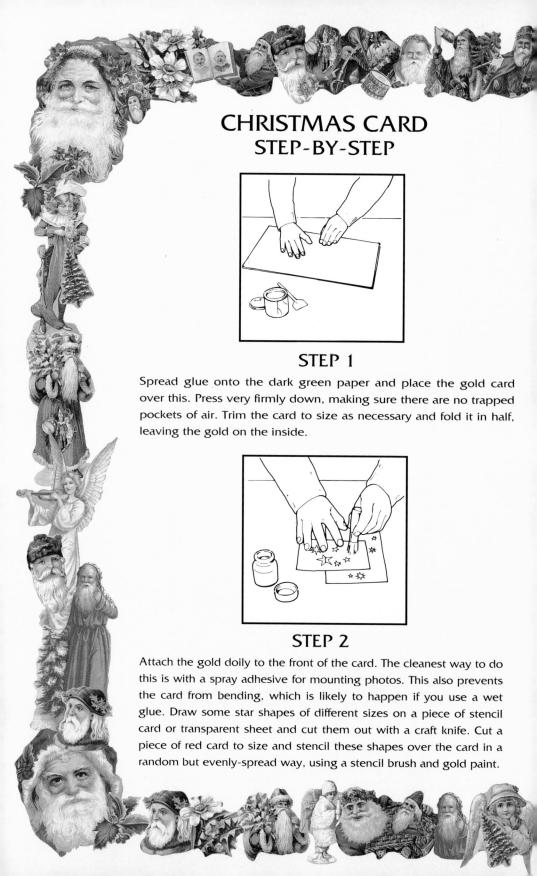

STEP 1

Spread glue onto the dark green paper and place the gold card over this. Press very firmly down, making sure there are no trapped pockets of air. Trim the card to size as necessary and fold it in half, leaving the gold on the inside.

STEP 2

Attach the gold doily to the front of the card. The cleanest way to do this is with a spray adhesive for mounting photos. This also prevents the card from bending, which is likely to happen if you use a wet glue. Draw some star shapes of different sizes on a piece of stencil card or transparent sheet and cut them out with a craft knife. Cut a piece of red card to size and stencil these shapes over the card in a random but evenly-spread way, using a stencil brush and gold paint.

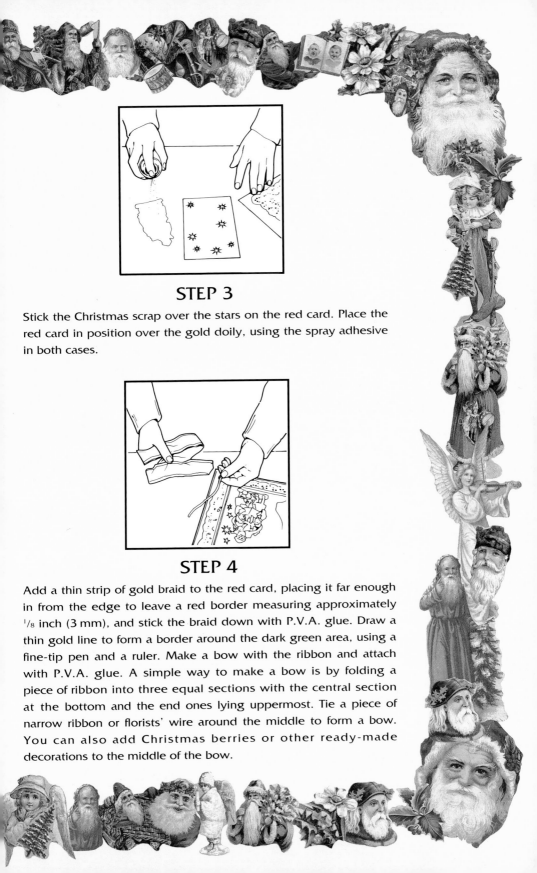

STEP 3

Stick the Christmas scrap over the stars on the red card. Place the red card in position over the gold doily, using the spray adhesive in both cases.

STEP 4

Add a thin strip of gold braid to the red card, placing it far enough in from the edge to leave a red border measuring approximately ¹/₈ inch (3 mm), and stick the braid down with P.V.A. glue. Draw a thin gold line to form a border around the dark green area, using a fine-tip pen and a ruler. Make a bow with the ribbon and attach with P.V.A. glue. A simple way to make a bow is by folding a piece of ribbon into three equal sections with the central section at the bottom and the end ones lying uppermost. Tie a piece of narrow ribbon or florists' wire around the middle to form a bow. You can also add Christmas berries or other ready-made decorations to the middle of the bow.

- PROJECT TEN -
CHRISTMAS TREE DECORATIONS

Christmas is a time of fun and celebration involving the whole family and there is infinite pleasure to be had in creating your own unique decorations. This project is simple enough to involve even young children: just watch the pleasure on their faces when they hang their own creations on the tree! If you can only find coloured papers and not card, stick some plain white card onto the back of the paper to stiffen it. You can, of course, replace the traditional colours used here with others that may be more appropriate to your decorative scheme - for example replacing the gold card and braid with silver. If you like, you can also paint the back of the decorations, so that they look attractive from all angles.

YOU WILL NEED

*Items from the basic materials kit
on page 8 plus*

Scraps from Sheets 57, 58, 59

Gold card

Burgundy card

Gold fine-tip marking pen

Narrow gold braid

Hole punch

Sticky tape

CHRISTMAS TREE DECORATIONS
STEP-BY-STEP

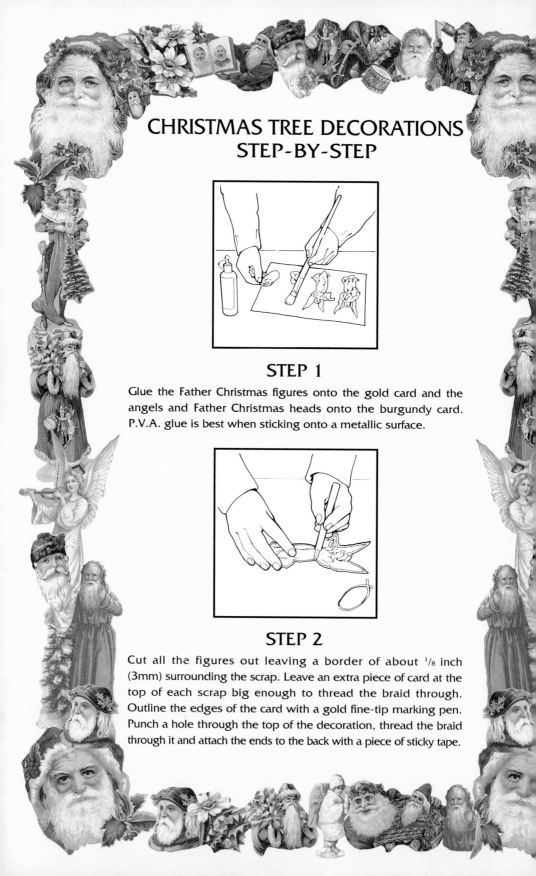

STEP 1

Glue the Father Christmas figures onto the gold card and the angels and Father Christmas heads onto the burgundy card. P.V.A. glue is best when sticking onto a metallic surface.

STEP 2

Cut all the figures out leaving a border of about ¹/₈ inch (3mm) surrounding the scrap. Leave an extra piece of card at the top of each scrap big enough to thread the braid through. Outline the edges of the card with a gold fine-tip marking pen. Punch a hole through the top of the decoration, thread the braid through it and attach the ends to the back with a piece of sticky tape.